This
coloring book
belongs to:
____

Copyright ©2020 TheInkElephant Press. All rights reserved. No part of this publication may be reproduced, distributed, or transmitted in any form or by any means, including photocopying, recording, or other electronic or mechanical methods, without the prior written permission of the publisher, except in the case of brief quotations embodied in critical reviews and certain other noncommercial uses permitted by copyright law.

Swainson's Lorikeet

Purple Naped Lory

Senegal Parrot

Blue Crowned Parakeet

Yellow Crowned Parakeet

Palm Cockatoo

Black Capped Lory

Orange Winged Amazon

Plum Headed Parakeet

Senegal Parrot

Bauer's Parakeet

Cuban Macaw

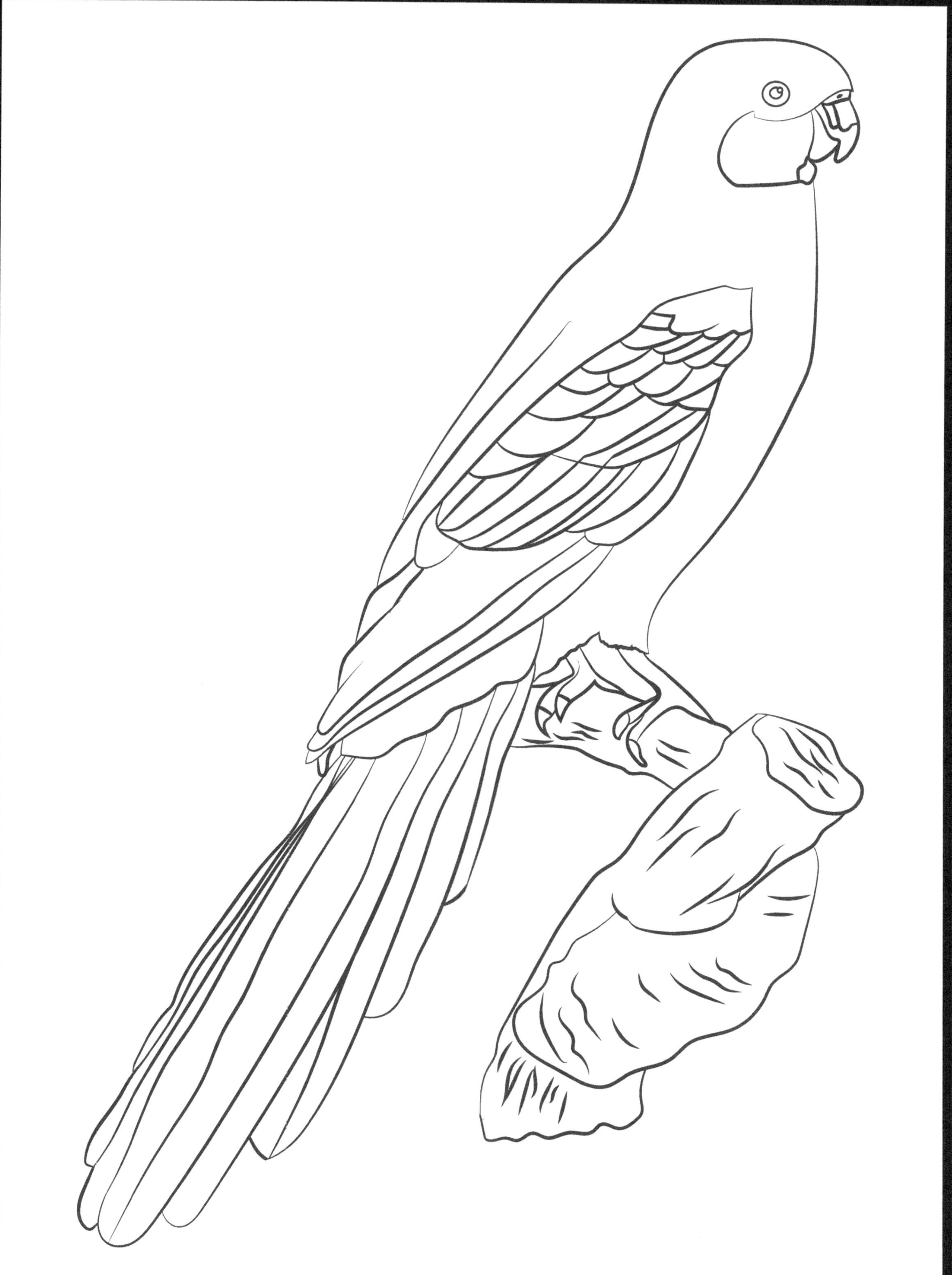

Crimson Rosella

Blue Crowned Lorikeet

Salmon Crested Cockatoo

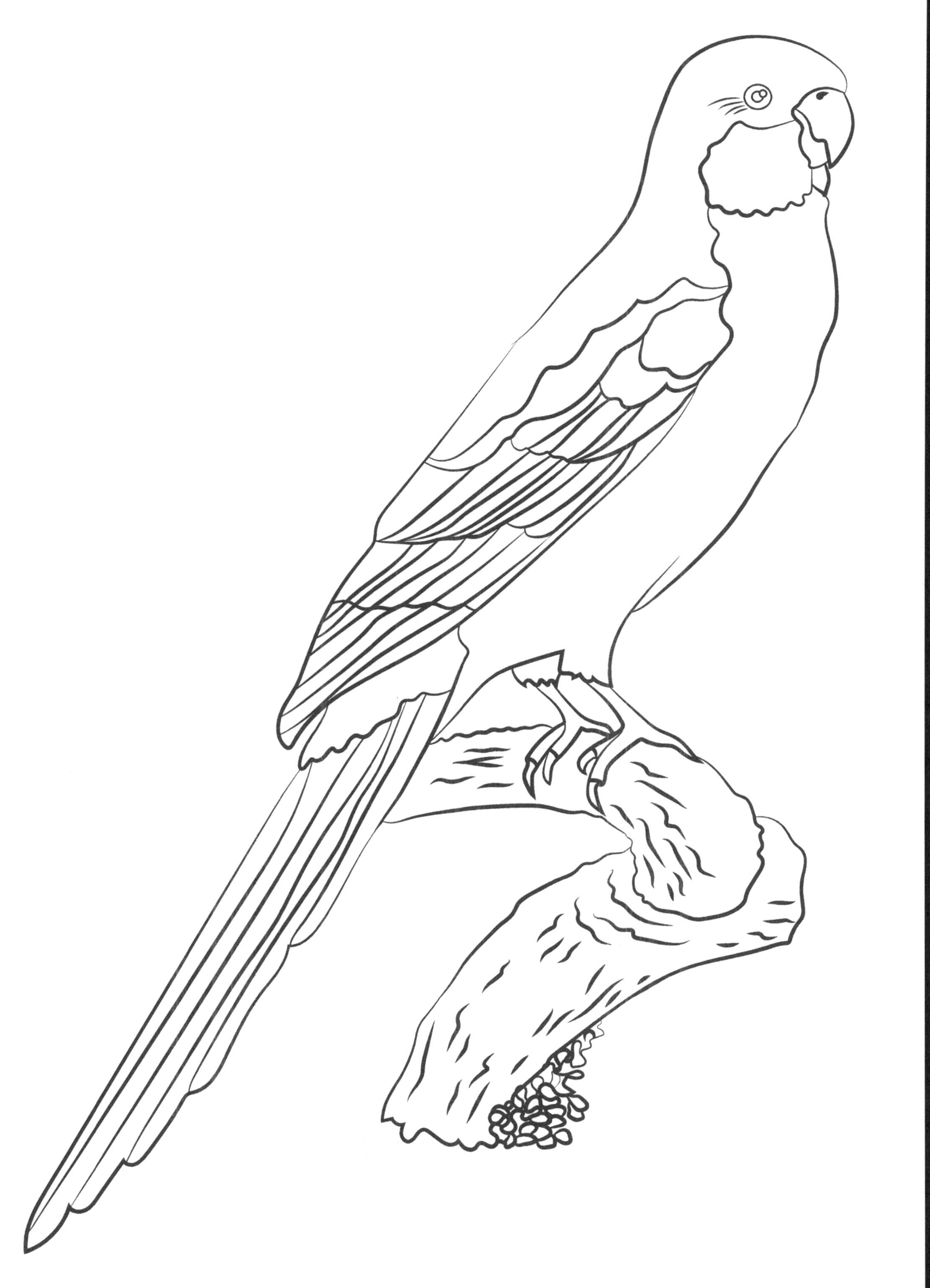

Broad Tailed Parrot

Violet Necked Lory

Blue Tipped Lory

Orange Cheeked Parrot

Blue Naped Parrot

Red Breasted Parakeet

Arimanon Parakeet

Marigold Parakeet

Turquoise Fronted Amazon

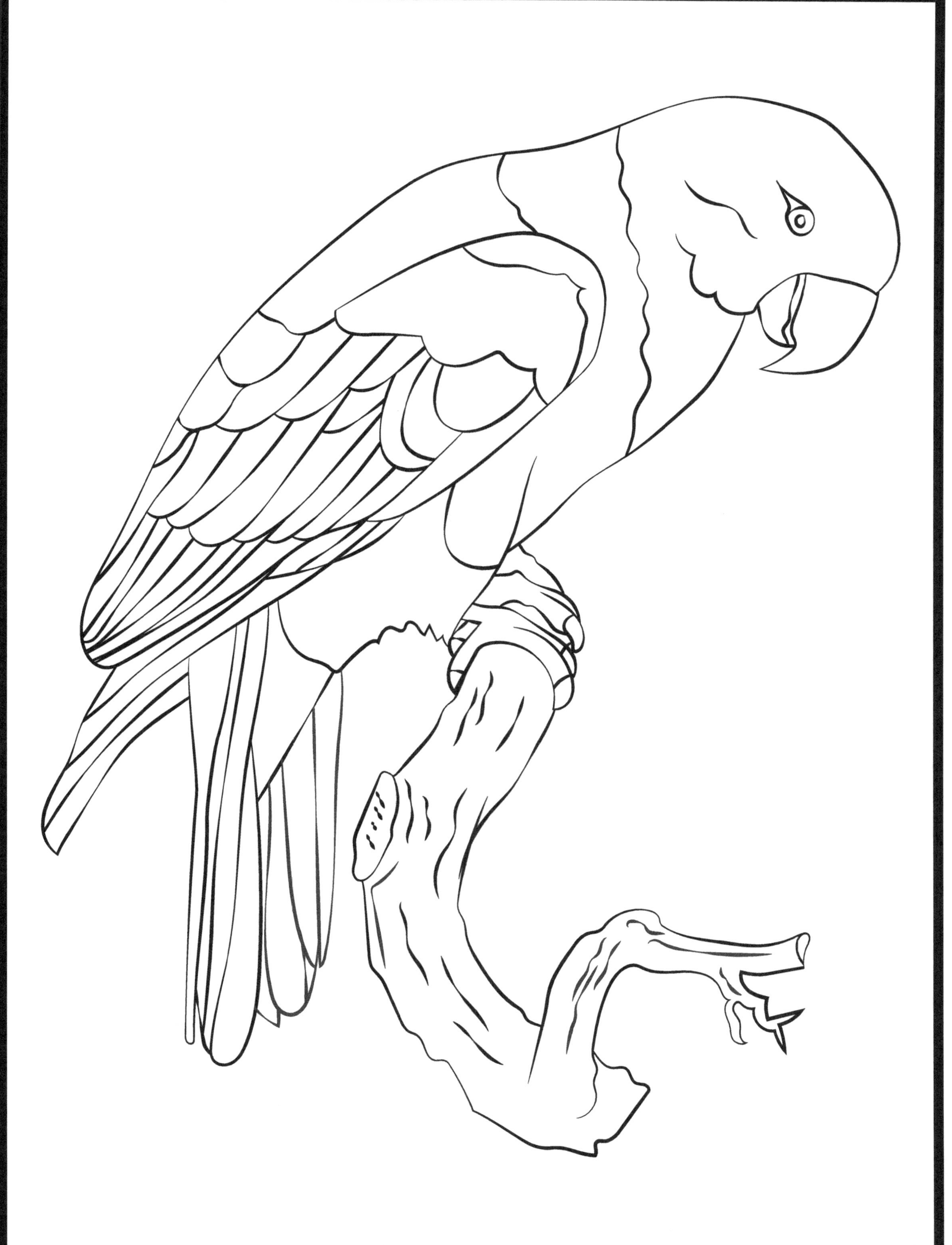

The Eclectus Parrot

Red Necked Amazon

Senegal Parrot

Peach Fronted Parakeet

Red Cheeked Parrot

Warbling Grass Parakeet

www.ingramcontent.com/pod-product-compliance
Lightning Source LLC
Chambersburg PA
CBHW081600270726
48657CB00029B/3414